T0024758

Technology through the Ages

MACHINES
THROUGH THE AGES
From Furnaces to Factories

MICHAEL WOODS AND MARY B. WOODS

TWENTY-FIRST CENTURY BOOKS™ / MINNEAPOLIS

For Orion Woods-Powders

Twenty-First Century Books™
An imprint of Lerner Publishing Group, Inc.
241 First Avenue North
Minneapolis, MN 55401 USA

For reading levels and more information, look up this title at www.lernerbooks.com.

Main body text set in Bembo Std Regular
Typeface provided by Monotype Typography.

Library of Congress Cataloging-in-Publication Data

Names: Woods, Michael, 1946– author. I Woods, Mary B. (Mary Boyle), 1946– author.
Title: Machines through the ages / Michael Woods and Mary B. Woods.
Description: Minneapolis : Twenty-First Century Books, [2024] I Series: Technology
    through the ages I Includes bibliographical references and index. I Audience: Ages
    11–18 I Audience: Grades 7–9 I Summary: "Ancient civilizations accomplished great
    works of engineering without electricity. From the Great Wall of China to Machu
    Picchu, discover the machines ancient civilizations used to build wonders and how
    they formed the foundation for modern machines"— Provided by publisher.
Identifiers: LCCN 2023010765 (print) I LCCN 2023010766
    (ebook) I ISBN 9798765610053 (lib. bdg.) I ISBN 9798765625224 (pbk.) I
    ISBN 9798765619452 (eb pdf)
Subjects: LCSH: Machinery—History—Juvenile literature. I BISAC: YOUNG ADULT
    NONFICTION / Technology / Machinery & Tools
Classification: LCC TJ147 .W665 2024 (print) I LCC TJ147 (ebook) I DDC 621.809—
    dc23/eng/20230323

LC record available at https://lccn.loc.gov/2023010765
LC ebook record available at https://lccn.loc.gov/2023010766

Manufactured in the United States of America
1 – CG – 12/15/23

CONTENTS

INTRODUCTION

W hat do you think of when you hear the word *technology*? You probably think of computers, smartphones, and the latest scientific tools. But technology doesn't just mean brand-new machines and discoveries. Technology is as old as human civilization.

Technology is the use of knowledge, inventions, and discoveries to make life better. The word technology comes from two Greek words. *Tekhne* means "art" or "craft." The suffix *-logia* means the study of arts and crafts. In modern times, technology refers to a craft, a technique, or a tool itself.

People use technology to help make human life easier, safer, and more enjoyable. This book looks at a technology that has been used for all of these tasks: machines.

What Is a Machine?

A machine is a device that does work. Work usually involves doing or making something—accomplishing a task. But engineers have a special definition of work. To engineers,

4

This relief image, created around 2325 BCE, is from a tomb in the ancient Egyptian burial grounds of Saqqara. It shows two sculptors using hammers and chisels to carve a statue. Many ancient cultures depicted machines and tools in their artwork.

work means transferring energy from one object to another. This transfer of energy causes the object to move or change direction. When you swing a baseball bat or kick a soccer ball, you are moving energy from your body to the ball to change its direction and move it somewhere else. You have done work. The amount of work depends on the amount of force applied to the object and the distance the object moves.

Machines allow people to apply more force and do more work than could be done with muscle power alone. With machines, people can also apply force more efficiently.

Some machines get their power from motors with

hundreds of moving parts, such as cars. These machines often need an energy source to run, such as gasoline or electricity. Other machines are very basic. For example, scissors, tweezers, knives, and bottle openers are machines that also do work. But the energy they use does not come from fuel or electricity. Instead, the food we eat is turned into energy in our muscles which can be used to easily operate these simple machines.

Learning from the Past

Archaeologists study ancient machines to understand ancient people and how they used technology. Some machines still exist because they were built out of stone or metal. But most ancient machines made of wood, animal hide, or plant fibers rotted away long ago. We can still learn about these machines from ancient pictures or written descriptions.

Over time, scientists and engineers have improved on many ancient technologies. They have made machines faster, more precise, more powerful, and more durable. But some ancient machines haven't changed much. If you've ever used a wheelbarrow, you have used a technology developed in China more than two thousand years ago.

Simple and Complex

All machines, no matter how complicated they may seem, are made from some combination of six simple machines. The simple machines are the lever, the wheel and axle, the inclined plane, the pulley, the wedge, and the screw. Ancient peoples around the world used all six simple machines, from

axes to cut wood to pulleys to build monuments. They also combined different kinds of simple machines to create more complex devices. One such device was the Claws of Archimedes, which could lift battleships out of the water and smash them to pieces. Read on to discover how these and other machines help us understand the incredible feats of engineering in ancient civilizations.

Inuit people made this sled in the 1800s. Their building materials were driftwood and the bones and tusks of sea animals. Their ancestors probably built similar sleds.

CHAPTER ONE

Machine Basics

The first modern humans on Earth lived about 300,000 years ago. They lived in small groups and got their food by hunting game, fishing, and gathering wild plants. When the food in one area was all used up, the group moved to a new place. They made tools from stone, wood, animal bones, animal hides, plant fibers, and clay. The most common prehistoric tools were some form of simple machine, such as a lever or a wedge.

Top Toolmakers

Cro-Magnons, a group of early humans, were skilled toolmakers. They lived in Europe between thirty-five thousand and ten thousand years ago. Cro-Magnon craftspeople carved stone, animal bones, and animal horns into excellent tools. These tools include harpoons (barbed spears), spear-throwers, and needles. Needles enabled people to sew garments out of animal hides and furs. This clothing kept people warm, so they could live in harsh, cold climates. Cro-Magnon people certainly

needed this technology. They lived during the last ice age, which ended about ten thousand years ago. During this era, much of Europe was covered by sheets of ice.

Simple Machine: The Lever

A lever is a bar or beam used to lift objects or pry them loose. When you push down on one end of a lever, the other end can lift a load, such as a rock stuck in the ground. The lever pivots, or turns, on a support called a fulcrum. The first fulcrum was probably a rock on the ground. By placing a stick on top of a rock, a person can push down on one end of the stick. Doing so causes the stick to pivot against the rock and lifts the other end.

An oar in a boat is a type of lever. One end is the handle,

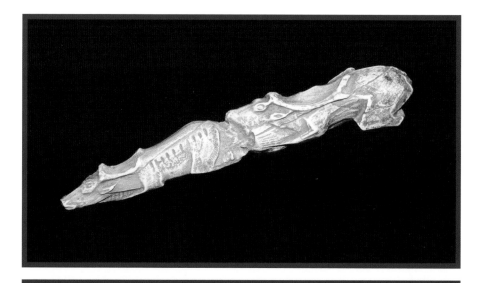

This ancient spear-thrower was found in Bruniquel, France. It is made of ivory and is estimated to be around 14,000 years old.

A modern Australian man shows how to use a spear thrower. The end of the spear sits in the thrower. When the man brings his arm forward, the spear shoots from the thrower with extra power and speed.

held by the person operating the oar. The side of the boat acts as a fulcrum. The oar's flat blade is the other end of the lever. The person rowing with the oar supplies the force in the form of muscle power. The moving blade pushes on the water, moving the boat.

A spear-thrower is another kind of lever. Ancient peoples around the world used wood or antler spear-throwers to propel spears and make them go farther. In North America, this was called an atlatl. The front end of the spear-thrower rested in a hunter's hand, along with the spear. When the hunter released the spear, the back end of the spear-thrower pushed the spear forward with extra force. With a spear-thrower, a hunter could propel a spear four times farther than using muscle power alone. The oldest known spear-throwers date from 15,000 to 11,000 BCE.

Simple Machine: The Wedge

A wedge is a piece of wood, stone, metal, or other material that is thicker at one end than at the other. Knives, axes, and chisels are all wedges. Our front teeth work as wedges to cut through food.

Imagine cutting an apple with a knife. The tip of the knife, the thinnest edge, begins to split the apple. As the knife moves deeper into the apple, the wider edge further splits the apple.

Prehistoric peoples made wedges out of stone to cut meat, grass, sticks, and bark. These wedges included axes, knives, and arrowheads. People made these tools by knapping, or knocking two stones together to chip pieces away. Through knapping, they were able to create tools with sharp edges. Flint was the best stone for toolmaking. Flint is a hard stone, but a skilled knapper could chip away at the edges of a piece of flint to create a smooth, sharp blade.

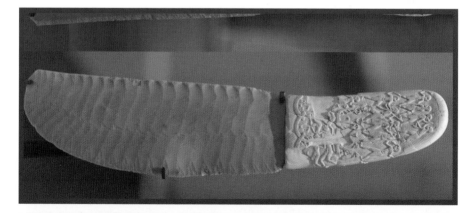

This knife was made in Egypt more than five thousand years ago. The handle is ivory, and the wedge-shaped knife blade is a hard stone called flint.

Stonecutting tools are even older than human society. Archaeologists have found knapped stone tools in Ethiopia that date from 1.5 to 2 million years ago, likely used by early hominids.

Bow Drills

A bow is a two-part machine that consists of a curved strip of material and a cord, called a bowstring, connecting one end of the strip to the other. Early peoples made bows from wood. The cord that connected the two ends was made from a vine, a string of animal hide, or an animal tendon. Archaeologists think that people first used bows more than thirty thousand years ago in northern Africa.

This wall painting is from the tomb of Rekhmire, a high Egyptian official serving the pharaoh in the 1400s BCE. Carpenters use a bow drill to make holes in a table or a bench.

When Was the Stone Age?

Historians sometime often refer to eras according to the kinds of tools people made. They talk about the Stone Age, the Bronze Age, and the Iron Age. This is called the three-age system. But these labels can be hard to define, because different groups used different materials for tool building at different times. For instance, the Middle East entered the Bronze Age about 3500 BCE. Greece entered the Bronze Age about 3000 BCE, and China around 1800 BCE. Because the three-age system was based on European prehistory, many historians argue it is not useful when describing cultures outside Europe.

When we think of bows, we usually think of bows and arrows used as weapons. But the first bows were probably drills. The bowstring was looped around a pointed shaft, such as a long, narrow stick or a stone. By moving the bow in a sawing back-and-forth motion, the operator could set the shaft spinning. The operator used the point of the spinning shaft to drill holes in wood, bone, or stone.

A bow drill's spinning movement creates friction at the tip of the drill. Friction occurs when objects rub together. Friction slows down moving objects and creates heat. You can experience friction yourself by pressing the palms of your hands together and rubbing rapidly.

Ancient peoples spun the shaft of a bow drill into a piece of wood until it began to smolder, or burn without a flame. Dry moss, leaves, or twigs added to the smoldering wood burst into flame.

CHAPTER TWO
The Ancient Middle East

A round 10,000 BCE, some people in the Middle East began to build settlements. They built villages and cities. Many people settled between the Tigris and Euphrates rivers in a region known as Mesopotamia. The area included most of modern Iraq and parts of modern Syria and Turkey.

Mesopotamia was home to ancient cultures over several thousand years. These included the Sumerians, Babylonians, Hittites, and Assyrians. These and other ancient Middle Eastern peoples created many useful machines.

Simple Machine: The Pulley

A pulley is a wheel with a grooved rim. The groove is designed to hold a rope or a chain. Imagine a tall pole with a pulley on top. A person threads a rope over the groove in the pulley and attaches a load to one end of the rope. By pulling on the other end of the rope, the person can lift the load more easily. Pulling down on a pulley uses body weight to give extra force to the pull. Ancient peoples probably first used pulleys to hoist buckets of water from wells.

14

An ancient Egyptian uses a shadoof to water plants. This modern painting is based on an original image from the tomb of a sculptor named Ipi in the ancient city of Thebes. The original picture dates to the 1200s BCE.

Simple Machine: The Wheel and Axle

Mention wheels, and most people think of round devices on cars, bicycles, and other vehicles. It's true that vehicles use wheels and axles. But doorknobs, wrenches, screwdrivers, steering wheels, and water faucets are made of wheels and axles too.

Wheels turn around a center shaft called an axle. Some modern water faucets are examples. They consist of a knob (the wheel) and a stem (the axle). Without the knob on

the faucet, it would be very hard to turn the smaller stem. That's because more force can be applied to a wheel, which has more surface area than an axle. That extra energy gets transferred to the smaller axle connected to it. That's how the knob of a faucet can move the stem with much less force than is needed to turn just the stem.

Putting the Wheel and Axle to Work

The Mesopotamians made the first wheeled vehicles around 3500 BCE. These were two- or four-wheeled wooden carts.

Horses pull a wheeled chariot in this stone carving from the Royal Tombs of Ur in modern-day Iraq. Archaeologists believe this carving to be one of the earliest known representations of the wheel.

People pulled the carts themselves or hitched them to oxen or other strong animals. The first pictures of wheeled carts are line drawings from the Sumerian city of Ur. They were drawn around 3200 BCE. Archaeologists have also found the remains of actual wooden wagons from Ur that were used sometime between 2600 and 2400 BCE.

Wheeled transportation revolutionized business, travel, warfare, and other aspects of ancient life. With wheeled vehicles, traders, armies, and other travelers could move more quickly and more efficiently. From Mesopotamia the wheel quickly spread to Europe, Africa, and Asia.

Spinning

About eleven thousand years ago, ancient peoples began to domesticate animals. Domesticated animals live among humans instead of in the wild. With domesticated sheep, people could cut off wool and turn it into cloth. Turning wool into cloth requires a technology called spinning.

Most natural fibers are very short. Cotton fibers, for instance, are only about 0.5 inches (1.25 cm) long. Spinning changes short pieces of fiber into long strands of thread or yarn. People can weave or knit the strands together to make fabric.

Mesopotamians used machines called the spindle and the distaff to turn sheep's wool into yarn. The distaff is a small stick with a slot on one end. The slot holds clumps of wool. The spindle is a long straight stick held between the thumb and index finger. By twirling the spindle, a person can carefully draw fibers off the distaff. The short wool fibers cling and twist together. They become a long strand of yarn.

India Did It First

People in ancient India made the first spinning wheel. Instead of a small whorl, this machine had a large wheel to turn the spindle. The invention dates to 500 BCE.

The ancient Indians also were among the first people to use steel. Steel is iron with extra carbon added to it. In ancient India, blacksmiths would heat the raw iron and hammer it until the impurities fell away. They would then wrap it in wood so that some of the carbon from the charred wood would mix into the iron. The extra carbon made the steel stronger and more durable than ordinary iron.

A modern-day woman from India uses a spinning wheel similar to the ones used throughout the ancient world.

Ancient peoples attached their spindles to small disks called whorls. The whorl adds more mass so when the spindle is spun, the added energy from that moving mass keeps the spindle in motion much longer. Whorls could be made of many different materials, including clay, bone, and metal.

The Potter's Wheel

Pottery making is a very old technology. The first evidence of pottery making comes from ancient Japan. People there made pottery as early as 14,000 BCE. For centuries the primary tool for pottery making was the human hand. People pinched balls of clay into the shape of a bowl or jar. Or they rolled out long ropes of clay and coiled them to create the walls of a pot. Potters fired the vessels in hot ovens to harden the clay.

Around 3500 BCE, about the same time people started using wheels for transportation, people in Mesopotamia developed the potter's wheel. The first potter's wheel was probably just a simple wooden circle that could be turned slowly on the ground as the potter coiled clay into a pot or bowl. The turning wheel allowed the potter to stack the coils faster and more evenly.

Ancient peoples soon built heavier and faster turntables made from stone. They probably greased the axles to reduce friction. With less friction, a wheel could move easier and last longer. Potters put a lump of wet clay onto the wheel, spun the wheel, and used their hands to form the spinning clay into a pot. This technique was called throwing. One of the earliest images of ancient pottery throwing comes from an Egyptian tomb from 1879 BCE.

Metals Make Better Machines

Ancient peoples used metals to make more powerful and efficient machines. Metals are stronger and last longer than stone, bone, and wood. They also have a property called plasticity. Plasticity is the ability to be melted, bent, stretched, shaped, and reshaped without breaking.

Ancient bronze was an alloy, or mixture, of copper and tin. It is made by melting these metals in a furnace, mixing them together, and allowing the mixture to cool. Craftspeople in Mesopotamia and Anatolia (modern-day Turkey) began making bronze in the 3000s BCE. They found that bronze was harder, stronger, and more durable than pure copper. It also could be easily cast. Casting involves melting metal into liquid form, pouring it into a mold, and

An Egyptian model from around 2500 BCE shows a potter throwing pots on a wheel.

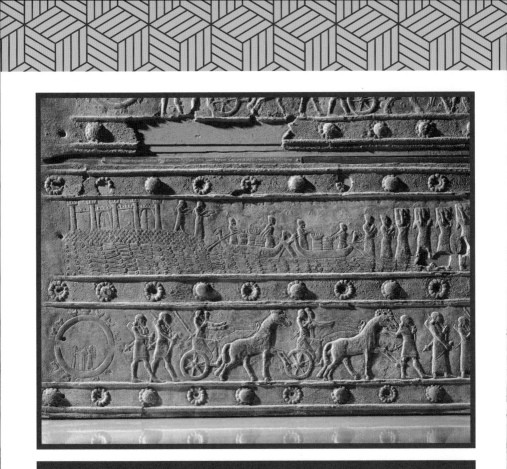

This is one of thirteen bronze panels that were nailed to the gates of the Assyrian Temple of Mamu in modern-day Iraq. The scenes commemorate important events of the day in the 800s BCE. These cast bronze panels are on display at the British Museum in London.

allowing it to harden. When an ancient bronze tool broke, a craftsperson could recycle the metal by melting it and recasting it into another tool. Peoples in the ancient Middle East made bronze tools, weapons, and armor.

Iron is stronger and harder than bronze. In about 1200 BCE, the Hittites began to make iron-tipped spears and battle-axes. These weapons gave them an advantage over enemies who had softer bronze weapons.

Making iron tools was hard for people in the ancient

Middle East. If they wanted to cast iron, they had to melt it first. Iron melts at about 2,800°F (1,538°C). But the furnaces in the ancient Middle East could not reach that temperature. So Middle Eastern craftspeople found another way to work with iron. They heated it in furnaces to soften it. When the iron was red hot, a craftsperson pulled it from the furnace and pounded it into shape using heavy hammers. Iron shaped by pounding is called wrought iron.

The First Machine Tool

Craftspeople use machine tools to cut and shape metal and wood. Archaeologists think the first machine tool was the lathe from the ancient Middle East. Lathes are used to shape objects into a circular form around an axis. For example, someone may use a lathe to carve decorative, rounded wooden legs for chairs and other furniture. A person using a lathe first places the object, such as a square piece of wood, on a spindle. As the spindle rotates, the object rubs against a sharp blade. The blade peels and scrapes away excess wood, giving the object the desired rounded shape.

We do not know exactly when the lathe was invented. Some evidence comes from ancient Turkey and dates to the 800s BCE. It includes objects apparently shaped by a lathe. Carvings and paintings from other parts of the ancient Middle East show furniture that was probably cut with lathes.

CHAPTER THREE
Ancient Egypt

ncient Egypt is famous for its giant pyramids. The pyramids are tombs of Egyptian pharaohs, or rulers. The largest, the Great Pyramid of Giza, is the tomb of Pharaoh Khufu. It was built around 2600 BCE. The Great Pyramid of Giza is 481 feet (147 m) high. Each side of its base is 756 feet (230 m) long. Builders used two million blocks of limestone to make the pyramid. Most of the blocks weighed about 3.5 tons (3.2 t).

When they built the pyramids, the Egyptians probably knew about only three simple machines. These were the lever, the wedge, and the inclined plane. How did the Egyptians build such massive pyramids with only three simple machines?

Simple Machine: The Inclined Plane

An inclined plane is a flat surface that slopes up and down. It sounds so simple that it might be hard to believe an inclined plane is really a machine. But the inclined plane is one of the

The Pyramids of Giza were built as tombs for pharaohs in Egypt's Old Kingdom. The Great Pyramid (right) was built around 2600 BCE as a tomb for the pharaoh Khufu.

most important machines for lifting heavy loads. Pushing an object up an inclined plane requires less force than lifting that object up vertically. Many buildings have ramps alongside stairs that allow people to use wheelchairs or push carts to higher floors. Ramps are a type of inclined plane.

Archaeologists have found the remains of earthen ramps at several pyramid sites. They think builders used these inclined planes to drag blocks up to the top of the pyramid. As the pyramid rose higher, workers built the ramps higher. They tore the ramps down when the pyramid was finished.

This ramp helped the ancient Egyptians move huge slabs of stone hundreds of feet off the ground during the construction of the pyramids.

Mechanical Advantage

How helpful is a machine to a person lifting a load? Engineers answer that question by talking about mechanical advantage. Mechanical advantage is the amount of help a machine provides in doing work. For example, if a lever allows you to move a 200-pound (90 kg) stone with just 50 pounds (23 kg) of force, then the lever has multiplied your force by four. The mechanical advantage of that lever is four.

In the case of the inclined plane, mechanical advantage is equal to the length of the plane divided by the height the object must be raised. So if you needed to raise a refrigerator 6 feet (1.8 m) into a truck, a 6-foot ramp would be of no help. Its mechanical advantage (6 divided by 6) would be only 1. With an 18-foot (5.5 m) ramp, however, loading the refrigerator would be a breeze. The ramp's mechanical advantage would be 3 (18 divided by 6): for every 3 pounds (1.4 kg) of load, the mover would need to exert only 1 pound (0.5 kg) of force.

The ancient Egyptians used ramps that were hundreds— even thousands—of feet long. This was the only way to gain the mechanical advantage needed to move giant stones to great heights.

More Building Machines

Before ancient Egyptians could build pyramids, laborers had to cut large limestone slabs from stone quarries. Stonecutters invented a clever way of splitting the slabs. First, they inserted

Don't Believe Everything You Read

The Greek historian Herodotus (ca. 484–425 BCE) wrote about life in ancient Egypt. He wrote that one hundred thousand men built the Great Pyramid over twenty years. But modern archaeologists think the tomb was built faster and with fewer workers. The remains of the workers' barracks at the pyramid site show that it would have housed four thousand people.

Herodotus described events in Egypt about two thousand years after they happened. Any historian writing about events that happened so long ago is bound to make some mistakes. In addition, Herodotus got his information as a tourist would: he visited Egypt and talked to the local people. His information was only as accurate as the stories he had heard.

This Egyptian painting from around 1000 BCE shows workers dragging limestone blocks on a sledge.

wooden wedges into natural cracks or drilled a line of holes in the rock and drove wedges into the holes. Then workers soaked the wedges with water to make the wood swell and expand in the cracks and holes. The stonecutters later inserted larger wooden wedges. They repeated the process until the slab of rock broke free.

To move the big stone blocks to building sites, workers floated them on river barges. At construction sites, people probably dragged the stones on sledges, rectangular platforms that slide across the ground. Ancient Egyptians probably put narrow runners on the undersides of sledges to reduce friction. Less material touching the ground meant less friction. The sledge could move faster.

Who figured out how to cut giant stone slabs with wedges and move them using sledges, levers, and inclined planes? No one knows for sure. But Imhotep, adviser to Pharaoh Djoser, might have played a role. Around 2650 BCE,

Imhotep supervised construction of the Pyramid of Djoser at Saqqara. This was the first pyramid built in Egypt. Manetho, an Egyptian priest and historian, called Imhotep the "inventor of the art of building in hewn [cut] stone."

> "...from the summit of yonder pyramids forty ages behold you."
> —Napoleon Bonaparte

Beyond the Pyramids

Because of the pyramids, ancient Egypt has been associated with large-scale building projects. But Egyptians also worked with small machines to help them with day-to-day work.

While people in other ancient cultures used oars or paddles to power boats, the Egyptians probably invented the first rudders. The first rudders were flat wooden boards that helped people steer boats more effectively. Like oars and paddles, they are machines—specifically, levers. One end of the lever holds a handle, called a tiller. The other end of the lever sits in the water. The back edge of the boat acts as the fulcrum. When a sailor moves the tiller to the right or left, the other end of the rudder moves in the opposite direction. It presses against the water. This action turns the boat in one direction or the other. Archaeologists have found rudders on the remains of ancient Egyptian boats and models of boats. These artifacts show that rudders were common in ancient Egypt.

Another useful machine from ancient Egypt was the water clock, or clepsydra. Before this invention, ancient people used sundials to tell time. A sundial is a flat disk with a gnomon, or upright bar, in the center. When sunlight hits a sundial,

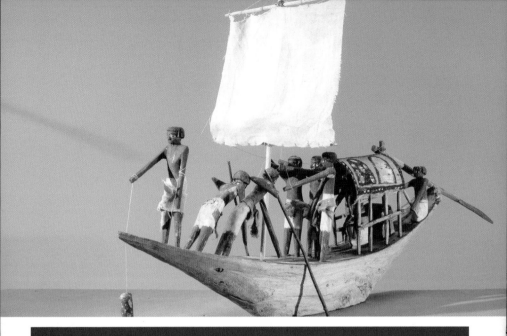

This model boat, complete with a rudder, was buried in a tomb around 1900 BCE. Boats inside tombs were supposed to transport dead people to the afterlife.

the shadow of the gnomon falls on a certain spot on the dial. As the earth rotates, the sun's position changes in the sky. As the sun's position changed, the shadow cast by the gnomon moved across the lines on the dial. Each line stood for a certain time of day. But the sundial didn't work at night or on cloudy days.

The clepsydra worked day or night. This simple device was made from a pottery jar. It had horizontal markings on the inside and a small hole at the bottom. At sunset a person filled the jar with water. The water flowed through the hole in the bottom of the jar at a constant rate. As the water dripped out, one marking after another became visible inside the jar. Each marking that appeared meant that an hour had passed. Ancient Egyptians built the first clepsydra around 1500 BCE. Water clocks spread from Egypt and became common in other ancient cultures.

Improving on the Loom

Looms are frames for using threads to weave cloth. Weavers start by connecting threads lengthwise across the loom. These threads are called the warp. They then interlace another set of threads across the warp. These threads are the weft. Archaeologists think that people in eastern Europe created the first looms around 6000 BCE. People in different cultures improved on the basic loom design. The ancient Egyptians, for example, added the heddle. This movable device keeps the threads of the warp separated from one another, making it easier to weave between them.

This modern painting is based on a scene originally created in the 1700s or 1600s BCE. The picture shows ancient Egyptians weaving (left) and spinning (right).

CHAPTER FOUR

Ancient China

T he ancient Chinese developed many technologies that are still important today. These include the printing press, paper making, and silk making. They also invented new devices, such as the blast furnace and bellows, that made other machines possible. These inventions allowed them to build larger projects. One was the Great Wall of China, which was built to protect the country from invaders. This landmark of construction technology runs for more than 13,000 miles (21,000 km) across northern China.

The Wooden Ox

The ancient Chinese invented one machine used all over the world today. One may be in your backyard. They called it the "wooden ox" or the "gliding horse." In English this machine is commonly called the wheelbarrow.

The wheelbarrow combines two simple machines: the lever and the wheel and axle. The platform and handles of the wheelbarrow make up the lever. When a person applies

The ancient Chinese built the Great Wall to keep out enemy invaders. Portions of the wall were built as early as the fifth century BCE. Most of the wall that still stands was built during the Ming Dynasty (1368–1644 CE).

force by lifting the handles, the platform lifts the load. The wheel and axle act as the fulcrum and pivot beneath the load, allowing the wheelbarrow to roll easily.

We do not know exactly which Chinese inventor gave us this machine. Some stories say that Chinese general Zhuge Liang invented the wheelbarrow around 230 CE. But wall paintings in the tomb of Emperor Liu Ying show people using wheelbarrows at least 100 years earlier.

The ancient Chinese used cast iron to make blades, handles, and other tools.

Casting Iron

People in the ancient Middle East could not get iron hot enough to melt. So they could not cast iron. Instead, they used wrought iron, which is weaker and less useful. The ancient Chinese were able to melt and cast iron.

In the 200s BCE, the ancient Chinese created a machine to assist them in casting iron. That machine was the hand-operated bellows. A bellows blows air through one end. It has a chamber that sucks in air and a valve for letting the air out. When a person presses on the air-filled chamber, air rushes out through the valve. These bellows produced strong currents of air, which contains oxygen. The oxygen fed the fire and made iron furnaces burn hotter.

Around 30 CE, a Chinese government worker named Du Shi invented a water-powered bellows. Power for the machine came from moving water, such as a river, that ran over a waterwheel. The water-powered bellows was much more powerful than hand-operated bellows and required less labor to operate.

Detecting Earthquakes

Modern scientists measure earthquakes with machines called seismometers. These instruments are extremely sensitive. They can detect movements one hundred thousand times smaller than the width of a human hair.

Zhang Heng, a Chinese scientist, built a similar device called a seismoscope in 132 CE. His machine could not measure ground movements, but it could tell people that an earthquake had occurred and in what direction. Zhang

A Better Bow

Like most early peoples, the ancient Chinese used bows and arrows for both hunting and warfare. In the 300s BCE, they invented the crossbow. A crossbow is more powerful than an ordinary bow. It has a crank or a lever for drawing back the bowstring and arrow. It pulls a stronger bowstring farther than an archer could on their own. The crossbow has advantages over ordinary bows. For one thing, crossbows exert more force than ordinary bows. This means crossbows can shoot arrows farther than ordinary bows. Those arrows strike with greater force.

In addition, crossbows have a catch to hold the bowstring in a cocked position. An archer can hold the bow, ready to shoot, as long as needed. With the catch doing the work of holding the bowstring, the archer doesn't have to hurry to take a shot. With plenty of time to aim, the arrow is more likely to hit the target.

Heng called his seismoscope an earthquake weather vane. A weather vane is a device that shows the direction of the wind. The earthquake weather vane was a big jar measuring 6 feet (1.8 m) across. The top of the jar had eight carved dragon heads that each faced a main direction on the compass: north, south, east, west, northeast, southeast, northwest, or southwest. Each dragon held a ball in its mouth. Below the dragons, at the base of the jar, were eight carved toads. Each toad had an open mouth. When an earthquake occurred, one of the eight dragons released its ball into the mouth of the toad below. People noted which toad caught the ball to learn in which direction the earthquake had taken place.

This model shows what Zhang Heng's earthquake weather vane might have looked like.

A Chinese historian tells this story about the earthquake weather vane: "On one occasion one of the dragons let fall a ball from its mouth though no perceptible shock [earthquake] could be felt....But several days later a messenger arrived bringing news of an earthquake in Lung-Hsi [400 miles (644 km) away]. Upon this, everyone admitted the mysterious power of the instrument."

Ancient writers didn't explain what happened inside the jar to trigger the balls to fall. Modern scientists think the jar contained an upside-down pendulum. This was a thin spike that was attached to the bottom of the jar but swung freely at the top. When there was an earthquake, the pendulum moved in the direction of the shaking and pushed a ball out of one of the dragon's throats.

CHAPTER FIVE

The Ancient Americas

O ver thousands of years, the Americas saw many civilizations and empires grow and develop machinery to accomplish great works of engineering. The tools they made were as diverse as the people. Materials ranged from wood, stone, bone, iron, copper, and bronze.

Copper working began in the Great Lakes region of North America as early as 5000 BCE. Copper was used for tools as well as for art. By 1000 BCE, people in the Andes Mountains of South America were smelting copper from ore to create ceremonial masks for burial. The Inuit people, who live in the arctic regions of North America and Greenland, made knives and spearheads out of iron as early as the eighth century CE.

Not every ancient American society relied on metals, though. The Aztecs, based in modern-day Mexico, made war clubs called macuahuitls out of wood, with edges of small, sharp obsidian pieces. Obsidian is a natural glass formed when volcanic lava cools rapidly. These obsidian blades could be made sharper than steel razors.

The Inca built magnificent cities, such as Machu Picchu in Peru, with only three of six simple machines.

Throughout the Americas, ancient peoples made other machines very similar to those made in ancient Africa and Eurasia. Spindles and whorls to spin yarn were made from stone, bone, or wood. Looms were made to weave elaborate textiles. They were even able to perform a type of brain surgery using early metal surgical tools.

The Wheel in the Americas

Like other early peoples, ancient

"[Their] arms consisted in shields of different sizes, sabres, and a species of broadsword, which is wielded with both hands, the edge furnished with flint stones, so extremely sharp that they cut much better than our Spanish swords."

—Spanish soldier Bernal Diaz del Castillo, describing Aztec weapons, 1568

39

A sixteenth-century Spanish chronicler made this drawing of Aztec warriors dressed in eagle and jaguar outfits and wielding macuahuitls.

Americans relied on simple machines to get work done. They used wedges, such as knives and chisels, and levers, such as digging sticks and paddles. The ancient Inca, who ruled a vast empire in South America, also used the inclined plane. Like the ancient Egyptians, the Inca built earthen ramps for hauling stone blocks high into place at construction projects. One of the

Wheeled toys such as this ceramic dog from pre-Columbian El Salvador show that Mesoamericans knew about wheeled transportation.

most famous was the huge mountaintop city of Machu Picchu in modern-day Peru.

Indigenous nations in the Americas did not build wheeled vehicles. This may have been because the Americas lacked large animals like horses and oxen to pull them. But there is evidence that people in ancient Mesoamerica (Mexico and Central America) understood the concept of the wheel. Archaeologists have found toy animals from ancient Mesoamerica with wheels on their legs. The toys were made from clay and mostly in the shape of dogs, monkeys, and wild cats. They date from the early 200s CE.

Scar tissue around holes in ancient skulls like the one shown below are signs that ancient surgeons performed successful brain surgeries. Ancient surgeons used knives or bow drills to perform brain surgery.

MACHINES THROUGH THE AGES

Iron from Shooting Stars

Some of the iron that ancient Americans used to make tools came from meteorites. These are rocks that crashed into Earth from outer space. Meteorites contain an easily usable form of iron. One was the Cape York meteorite in Greenland. This iron was hammered without heat in a process called cold forging. Other iron came from natural iron deposits in the Earth itself.

Medical Machines

Brain surgery is a difficult and dangerous procedure. But that did not stop ancient societies from attempting it. And, amazingly, it sometimes worked! Archeologists have found skulls from ancient peoples around the world with holes that were cut intentionally. Some of the holes have smooth edges that mean the bone healed. The edges changed from jagged cuts to smooth new bone. It is proof that some patients lived for years after surgery. To perform brain surgery, the surgeon cut or drilled holes in the patient's skull in a process called trepanning. This allowed them to ease pressure on the brain from blood that had built up after a head injury. Trepanning was used to treat headaches and other ailments. The surgeon had to be careful to cut only through the skull and not into the brain. After the operation, the surgeon may have covered the hole in the skull with a shell.

Surgeons used different kinds of tools to cut through the skull. The bow drill was one of the most common. But the ancient people of Peru used their own tool, the tumi. The tumi was a curved metal knife made of copper or bronze. It made rectangular cuts in a hashtag shape. With that cut, the surgeon opened the skull by removing the central square. Using metalwork and basic machines and practicing medical care, the ancient peoples of Peru were able to help people survive difficult surgeries and live longer lives.

Ancient Americans used metal to create ornamental pieces and tools. This gold ornament dates to the Inca Empire (1200–1500 CE).

Get Up and Go

Some archaeologists think the Inca used logrollers to move heavy stones. This process would have involved rolling a stone over a series of logs. As the stone moved along, people would have moved logs from the back of the line to the front to keep it rolling.

Many ancient North Americans who lived in the Great Plains dragged their possessions from place to place on travois. This area extends from the Rocky Mountains to the Mississippi River. They used wooden frames made of two long poles with a net or wooden platform between them for carrying gear. People hitched dogs to the travois to pull the load.

Toboggans originated among the Algonquin people and other residents of ancient North America. Dogs or people on snowshoes could easily pull heavy loads on toboggans over snow, ice, or flat land.

Travois were used by Indigenous Americans as late as the nineteenth century.

CHAPTER SIX
Ancient Greece

Ancient Greece was home to great philosophers, writers, and artists. Some Greeks thought that engineering was a lowly craft. They thought it was beneath the dignity of educated people. This attitude didn't seem to discourage Greek builders and engineers, however. They invented some of the most impressive machines of ancient times.

Simple Machine: The Screw

Ancient Greek culture arose around 750 BCE. By this time, five of the six simple machines were already in use. The Greeks developed the sixth simple machine and used it in many technologies. This machine was the screw.

The screw is based on another simple machine, the inclined plane. The threads, or ridges, on a screw provide mechanical advantage, just as an inclined plane does. But instead of aiding movement in a straight line, the threads on a screw allow movement in a spiral.

People often use screws as fastening devices. Turning a

This detail from a Greek vase from the 700s BCE shows two blacksmiths using a furnace to heat metal for shaping.

screw produces a force that holds the two pieces of material together. People also use screws to lift loads. Some jacks that lift cars and other heavy objects off the ground are large screws.

Grapes and Olives

Olives and grapes were among the most common crops grown by ancient Greek farmers. The Greeks crushed grapes to make wine and olives to make olive oil. To crush these fruits, they

47

used a machine called a press. Early presses were operated by a windlass, a machine that uses a crank to move a rope around a shaft, making the shaft spin.

The ancient Greeks developed a better press called a screw press. It combined two simple machines, the screw and the lever. The screw portion of the press was mounted upright. Turning it put upward pressure on the lever. As the end of the lever being pushed by the screw moved up, the opposite end moved down. The downward-moving section of the lever squeezed olives or grapes inside a container.

Greek screw presses were large machines. Some of the biggest ones were turned by oxen. Others were operated by a

The ancient Greeks used screw presses and other technology to crush grapes into wine. Modern Greece is still a grape-growing region.

single person turning the screw. These presses squeezed much more juice and oil out of fruit than earlier, windlass-driven presses.

In the first century CE, a Greek inventor named Hero made the screw press even better. His press didn't have a lever. It used the screw to apply force directly to grapes and olives. Removing the lever reduced friction. This change made Hero's screw press more forceful and more efficient than earlier screw presses

Ancient R&D

Many twenty-first century advances in technology come from research and development (R&D) programs. In these programs, experts work together to study problems and find solutions. The experts set goals, run experiments, and do tests. The R&D process can lead to new and improved products, and better ways of making them.

One ancient Greek ruler named Dionysius the Elder might have started the world's first R&D program in Rhodes. In 399 BCE, Dionysius needed new weapons to prepare for war with Carthage, a powerful city-state on the northern coast of Africa.

"Then at daybreak he [Demetrius, later king of Macedon, near Greece] brought his engines into the harbour with the sound of trumpets and with shouts; and with the lighter catapults, which had a long range, he drove back those who were constructing the wall along the harbour, and with the ballistae [large crossbow] he shook or destroyed the engines of the enemy."

—Diodorus Siculus, Greek historian, first century BCE

Modern-day colored illustrations show what ancient Greek catapults looked like.

Legend says that Dionysius gathered together teams of military specialists to build new weapons to stockpile for the war. Dionysius's team made several new inventions. One was a new ship called the quadrireme. Another was one of the first catapults. A catapult uses a lever to hurl rocks, spears, arrows, and other missiles at an enemy. However, some historians think that catapults were around long before Dionysus. Historical documents from the seventh century BCE, for instance, describe stone-hurling machines.

A New Reliance on Engineers

In the third century BCE, Greek engineers developed a complex formula to design catapults. The formula stated that the width of one catapult part had to be 1.1 times the cube root of one hundred times the weight of the stone it hurled. Finding cube roots involves advanced math.

The need for smart mathematicians and skilled engineers to design catapults and other machines gave them more respect in Greek society. The Greek army needed specially trained soldiers to operate such weapons. These became some of the first elite teams of soldiers.

Archimedes: Pulleys and Levers

Archimedes was one of the most important ancient mathematicians and engineers. He lived in Syracuse, on the island of Sicily, in the 200s BCE. At the time, Syracuse was a Greek colony. As a mathematician, Archimedes laid the foundation for calculus. This kind of math is used in medicine, engineering, computer games business, and many other fields. Archimedes discovered the basics of this system, including how to figure the area and the volume of cylinders and spheres. He described many mathematical techniques in a book called *The Method*.

Archimedes also invented important machines. One was a screw-like device for pumping water from rivers, lakes, and irrigation channels. Now called the Archimedes screw, it was a hollow shaft with a spiral tube inside. By rotating the shaft with a crank, a person could pump water from the bottom of the tube to the top.

There is evidence that Archimedes also invented the compound pulley, or block and tackle. A block and tackle is a combination of two different types of pulleys. The pulley

This diagram shows how the Archimedes screw can be used to transport water to a higher location.

at the top of a flagpole, for instance, is usually a fixed pulley. Fixed pulleys don't increase the pulley's lifting power. They simply change the direction of force. By pulling downward with a fixed pulley, a person lifts a load upward

Another type of pulley is a movable pulley. In this device, a load is attached to the grooved wheel of the pulley. A rope passes through the groove. One end of the rope is tied to a fixed support above the load (for example, a hook on a ceiling). A person pulls on the other end of the rope to lift the load. A movable pulley has a mechanical advantage of two. It doubles the force of a person's pull.

A block and tackle combines a fixed pulley with movable pulleys. The fixed pulley is attached to a support, such as a strong hook in an overhead beam. This pulley changes the direction of force. One movable pulley is attached to the load. Other movable pulleys are attached to ropes in between. The mechanical advantage of a compound pulley depends on the number of pulleys. The more pulleys the device has, the greater the mechanical advantage.

Archimedes studied levers and proved a theory called the law of the lever. The law shows how a lever can lift loads of different weights with the same amount of force by adjusting the position of the fulcrum. As the load increases, the lever's length must also increase to provide the necessary lifting force. After discovering the law, Archimedes boasted that with a long enough lever and a place to stand, he could move the world.

Plutarch, a Greek historian who lived during the first century CE, wrote a story about the Greek king Hiero II of Syracuse. Hiero II heard about Archimedes's boast and challenged him to single-handedly launch a huge warship from the dry dock where it had been built. Without machines, Hiero II would have needed hundreds of strong workers with ropes. But Archimedes did the job by himself. He built a system of compound pulleys that allowed him to move the ship while sitting comfortably in a chair on the dock. All he had to do was pull on some ropes.

The War Machines of Archimedes

The ancient Romans tried to capture Syracuse in 214 BCE. The Romans planned to set covered ladders against the city walls. Then soldiers would swarm over the top of the walls and into Syracuse.

Water and Air Power

Ctesibius was an inventor and a physicist who lived in Alexandria, Egypt, in the 100s BCE. At the time, Alexandria was ruled by the Greeks. He studied pneumatics, the science of compressed air. He also studied hydraulics, the science of liquids in motion. He learned how to use both air and water to power machines. His inventions include air pumps, water pumps, and water-driven musical instruments.

Ctesibius also improved on the Egyptian water clock. His clock had a float that sat in a jar of water. A statue with a pointer was mounted on top of the float. As water dripped into the jar, the float moved up with the water level. The statue on the float pointed to lines on a column, showing the time.

Ctesibius wrote several books about his inventions and discoveries, but none of them survived to modern times. Most of what we know about Ctesibius comes from the works of other ancient writers, such as the Roman engineer Marcus Vitruvius.

But the Syracuse defenders had prepared well for the attack. At the time, Archimedes was serving as a military adviser to King Hiero II. Archimedes designed huge cranes, much like modern construction cranes. Like modern cranes, these machines could swivel, catch things, lift them high into the air, and drop or lower them to the ground. The cranes had pulleys and ropes pulled by oxen. The cranes easily lifted huge boulders and lead balls weighing 600 pounds (272 kg). When the Romans approached Syracuse in their ships, soldiers swung the ends of the cranes over the city walls. The cranes dropped the boulders and lead balls on the attacking ships and smashed them.

Soldiers also used a weapon called the Claws of Archimedes to defend Syracuse. This was another giant crane with ropes and pulleys. One end of the crane had a hook-like claw hanging on a rope. When the Romans attacked, the Syracuse defenders lowered the hook into the water. The hook snagged the hull of an approaching Roman ship. Then oxen and pulleys went into action. They pulled the rope and lifted the enemy ship right out of the water.

The Greek writer Plutarch (ca. 46–119 CE) wrote about these battles hundreds of years later. He gave this description of the Claws of Archimedes:

> The ships . . . were dashed against steep rocks that stood jutting out under the walls, with great destruction of the soldiers that were aboard them. A ship was frequently lifted to a great height in the air (a dreadful thing to behold) and was rolled to and fro, and kept swinging, until the mariners [sailors] were all thrown out, when at length it was dashed against the rocks, or was let fall.

Getting Into Gear

The world's first known description of gears and gear trains dates to the 300s or 200s BCE. Gears are a variation on the wheel and axle. They transfer motion from one turning shaft to another turning shaft. The first gears were wooden wheels with small spokes projecting from the rim. These spokes fit together with spokes in another wheel. The motion of the first wheel turned the second wheel.

No one knows who made the first gears, but they were

55

widely used in ancient times. Ancient Greek engineers were fascinated with gears. They learned that gears could do more than just transfer motion. They could also change the direction, force, and speed of motion. For example, a small gear turning a larger gear increases force. A large gear turning a smaller gear increases speed. Gears can also be combined into gear trains to achieve various combinations of speed, force, and direction.

The Antikythera Mechanism

One day in 1901, divers were searching the seafloor near the Greek island of Antikythera. They were looking for natural sponges, but they discovered the wreck of an ancient cargo ship instead. It had sunk about two thousand years earlier. The divers brought up many relics from the shipwreck. These included marble statues and pieces of bronze.

As archaeologists cleaned the bronze, they discovered a series of gears. The gears were precisely made. They were obviously the remains of a machine.

In the 1950s, British historian Derek de Solla Price began studying the machine. After years of work, he concluded that it was an astronomical calendar from ancient Greece. The device had more than thirty gears. It calculated the movements of the sun, the moon, and the planets.

De Solla Price built a model based on the ancient gears. He found that the machine looked much like an analog clock. It probably had been housed inside a wooden case with a door.

In 2006 scientists took a closer look at the Antikythera Mechanism. Using three-dimensional X-ray scanners and

56

This is one of the bronze gears from the Antikythera Mechanism, which was built in the second century BCE. The mechanism was recovered from the bottom of the sea in 1901. The device used a series of bronze gears to perform astronomical calculations.

other imaging machines, they made several new discoveries. There were previously unknown inscriptions on the gears. The machine also contained calendars based on the movements of the sun and the moon. They concluded that the machine was built between 150 and 100 BCE. The new research proved that it was more advanced than previously believed. It could even predict solar and lunar eclipses.

CHAPTER SEVEN

Ancient Rome

Ancient Roman engineers used machines to build roads, bridges, aqueducts, mills, and weapons. They took ideas about geometry and trigonometry, developed by the ancient Greeks, and put them to practical use in construction projects.

A New Prime Mover

A prime mover is a machine that transforms heat, wind, or flowing water into mechanical energy that can power other machines. Prime movers often rotate a shaft, which then turns a wheel or a gear. Prime movers use energy to provide more force than a human or animal could provide.

Human muscles were the first sources of mechanical energy. At first, humans ate plants and animal meat, turning their nutrients into muscular energy they used to power wheels and other machines. Then humans began to use animals to operate machines, such as turning large mills or carrying heavy loads. Oxen were especially important to ancient peoples in Europe, Africa, and Asia due to their strength. It took thousands of years for people to develop the first prime mover that turned energy from nature into mechanical energy. This new prime mover was probably the waterwheel.

The Greek Mill

Early peoples used waterwheels to grind wheat and other grains into flour. Ancient Greeks made the first waterwheels in the first century BCE. These were wooden wheels with six to eight scoops connected to a central shaft. The wheel sat horizontally in

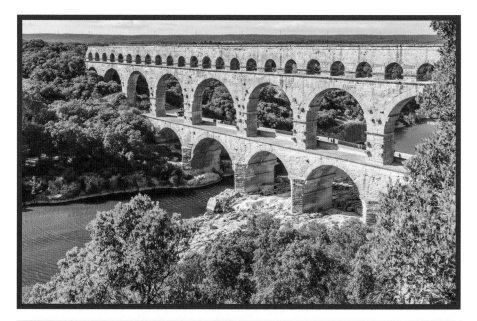

Aqueducts like the one shown above carried water from mountains to nearby Roman cities.

a fast-running stream. Water rushed into the scoops, turning the wheel and the central shaft. The shaft was connected to gears, which spun and turned millstones. The moving stones crushed grain into flour. The ancient Greek mill was not very efficient. It probably took several hours to grind 100 pounds (45 kg) of grain.

The Roman Mill

Roman engineers copied and improved these Greek mills. They converted the horizontal waterwheel into a vertical (upright) waterwheel.

This page from Marcus Vitruvius's *On Architecture*, written around 25 BCE, shows his design for a water-powered grain mill.

The Romans made two kinds of vertical waterwheels, the undershot and overshot wheels. The undershot wheel had blades that dipped into moving water. Water pushed the blades and the wheel turned. The overshot wheel was more efficient. It used a chute (a type of slide) to pour water over the top of the wheel. Both the current of the river and the weight of the falling water turned the wheel. Water is heavy. One gallon weighs about 8 pounds (0.9 kg/L). The weight of the falling water made the overshot wheel turn faster than the undershot wheel.

"Wheels on rivers are constructed upon the same principles as those just described. Round their circumference [outer rims] are fixed paddles, which, when acted upon by the force of the current, drive the wheel round, receive the water in the buckets, and carry it to the top."

—Marcus Vitruvius, *On Architecture*, first century BCE

The ancient Roman mill was a powerful new prime mover. Experts estimate that even the most basic Roman mill could grind thousands of pounds of grain a day. Yet the ancient Romans rarely used the mill on a wide scale. Of the three hundred grain mills in the city of Rome during the 200s CE, only a few were powered by water.

An Ancient Factory

France was once part of the vast Roman Empire. In southern France, archaeologists have found the remains of sixteen stone buildings with waterwheels. Archaeologists think the site was a huge factory for milling grain. It was built in the 300s CE. An

inscription on a nearby tomb suggests that an engineer named Quintus Candidius Benignus built it. The inscription praises him for being "clever like none other, and none surpassed him in the construction of machines."

The stone buildings stood in two parallel rows of eight buildings each. Both rows ran down the slope of a hill. Each building had its own waterwheel. Two channels of water ran down the hill, cascading onto the first wheel, then the next, and then the next. After turning the final wheel, the water ran into a drain and out to a marshy area about 0.25 mile (0.4 km) away.

Archaeologists estimate that the sixteen waterwheels produced enough power to grind about 9,900 pounds (4,491 kg) of flour each day. That flour could have fed about 12,500 people. The mill probably produced flour for the nearby city of Arles, which had a population of about 12,000 at the time.

The ancient factory probably produced no more than thirty horsepower. That's equal to about two riding lawn mowers. But experts believe that it had the greatest concentration of mechanical power in ancient Europe.

Going Up

The ancient Romans were famous for moving water. They built a series of aqueducts to carry water from mountain springs and lakes into big cities. Most aqueducts were elevated structures. They looked like bridges and spanned both land and water. The aqueducts sloped slightly downward. The downward slope allowed gravity to pull water down through the channels so that it flowed into cities.

Sometimes, however, the Romans and other ancient

In the 300s CE, water ran downhill and turned waterwheels in sixteen stone buildings here in Barbegal, France. Only some of the ancient stones remain.

peoples needed to move water up, not down. They needed to raise water from wells or into elevated storage tanks. For this job, ancient peoples built enormous water-lifting devices. One part of the device sat in a river or a well. It contained big buckets for scooping up water. Next to the water source, people or animals turned a giant shaft. The shaft was connected to a series of gears. The turning gears moved a chain, which moved the buckets. When a bucket reached its highest level, its water drained out into an irrigation channel or a storage tank.

In addition to lifting water for drinking and farming, the ancient Romans used water-lifting machines to supply water to public baths. These gathering places were like modern-day spas. Romans bathed, swam, took saunas, exercised, and socialized there. The water for the facilities was stored in overhead cisterns, or tanks. Water-lifting machines carried it up.

Ancient Water Pumps

Ctesibius of Alexandria invented a water pump in the 200s BCE. This device consisted of two parallel bronze cylinders. Inside the cylinders were movable valves called pistons. When a person moved the pump handle, one piston sucked water up into the first cylinder while the other piston pushed the water down through the second cylinder. From the second cylinder, the water ran into a tank or a nozzle. This type of pump is called a force pump. The ancient Romans improved on Ctesibius's force pump. They built big force pumps to fight fires, drain water from ships, and bring drinking water up from wells.

The ancient Romans used water-lifting machines to carry water to public baths, such as this one in Herculaneum in western Italy. The town was destroyed by the eruption of Mount Vesuvius in 79 CE.

After the Ancients

F or centuries, these ancient machines were the best in the world. Gradually, however, inventors throughout history have been rediscovering these ancient technologies, adapting them, and improving upon them. Many of those advances happened during the Industrial Revolution (1733–1913). New machines began to change the world faster than ever. Scottish engineer James Watt, for instance, developed a new powerful prime mover in 1769—the steam engine.

Rediscovering some ancient machine technologies took thousands of years. In 1899 a Greek scholar cataloged some ancient religious manuscripts stored in Constantinople (modern-day Istanbul), Turkey. He noticed that one of the manuscripts had some ancient Greek "undertext" beneath the religious writing. This text had been scraped off and written over in the early 1200s, but it was still visible. With the help of a translator, the scholar realized that the undertext was written by Archimedes. The ancient parchment contained three books by Archimedes, including *The Method*. This

65

During the Industrial Revolution, people began to build machines that surpassed those of ancient times. James Watt's steam engine, on display at a German museum, is one example.

discovery was a major advance in understanding technology through the ages.

Reconstruction

Engineers around the world have been amazed by ancient machines. In the early 1900s, Erwin Schramm, a German military officer, reconstructed ancient catapults. He used the

original plans from Dionysius's engineers. Schramm found these devices to be extremely accurate.

Later in the twentieth century, engineers built steam engines based on designs by the Greek engineer Hero. They

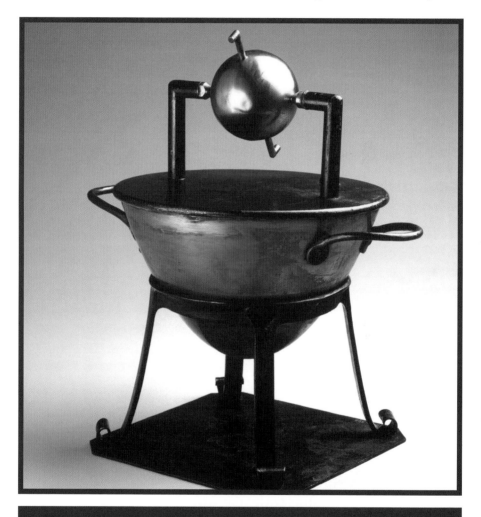

This working model shows how Hero's steam engine, the aeolipile, could have worked. The steam pushed out of the engine turns the ball-shaped turbine at the top.

Many museums give visitors a chance to interact with ancient technology firsthand, such as this re-creation of a Roman-era water-lifting machine.

found that Hero's engine could rotate up to fifteen hundred times per minute. Modern engineers have also reconstructed Greek warships, Roman mills, the Antikythera Mechanism, and other ancient machines.

Some museums display the remains of ancient machines alongside modern reconstructions. Visitors can even operate some reconstructed machines. For instance, the Museum of London in England built a full-size model of a two-thousand-

year-old Roman water-lifting machine. The replica was based on the remains of two real machines used in London when England was part of the Roman Empire. Modern visitors could push big wooden bars to turn the giant shaft that operates the machine. Engineers estimate that the original machine could have lifted 15,000 gallons (56,800 L) of water each day.

Reuse

The word *ancient* is sometimes used to mean old-fashioned or out of date. Many ancient machines do seem poorly suited to the modern world. After all, why travel by oxcart when you can take a car, a bus, a subway, or an airplane?

But a closer look tells a different story. Many ancient machines are still used in everyday life. Mortars and pestles that cooks use today are almost identical to those used more than 12,000 years ago in ancient Jordan.

Does your family have a wheelbarrow in the garage or backyard? If so, it probably looks a lot like the wooden ox and gliding horse built in ancient China in the first century CE. Although your wheelbarrow might be made from stronger and lighter materials, it combines the same two simple machines and operates on exactly the same mechanical basis as the ancient Chinese wheelbarrow.

Have you ever gone tobogganing in winter? Though many toboggans are now made with plastic, the design is nearly identical to that used by ancient Indigenous Americans. Hundreds and even thousands of years later, people still can't improve on some ancient machines.

TIMELINE

ca. 14,000 BCE   People in ancient Japan begin to make pottery.

ca. 10,000 BCE   People in the ancient Middle East begin farming.

ca. 6000 BCE   People in eastern Europe invent the loom.

ca. 3500 BCE   People in Mesopotamia create wheeled vehicles and the potter's wheel.

ca. 2600 BCE   Ancient Egyptians build the Great Pyramid of Giza.

ca. 1500 BCE   Ancient Egyptians build the clepsydra, or water clock.

ca. 1200 BCE   The Hittites smelt iron to create iron tools and weapons.

ca. 400 BCE   People in ancient China begin to cast iron.

390s BCE   Dionysius the Elder develops catapults to use in a war against Carthage.

300s BCE   People in ancient China invent crossbows.

200s BCE   The bellows is invented in ancient China. Archimedes invents machines and writes books on engineering, physics, and mathematics.

ca. 100 BCE   People in ancient Greece make the first waterwheel.

30 CE   Du Shi invents a water-powered bellows.

132   Zhang Heng builds a seismoscope.

ca. 300s   Romans build a milling factory in southern France.

1733   The Industrial Revolution begins in Europe.

1899   Greek scholars discover an ancient manuscript containing *The Method* by Archimedes and other books.

1901	Greek divers discover the Antikythera Mechanism in a shipwreck.
1950s	Derek de Solla Price begins studying the Antikythera Mechanism.
2006	Archaeologists discover the Antikythera Mechanism could predict eclipses.
2021	A team of scientists at University College London creates a new and more accurate model of the Antikythera Mechanism.

GLOSSARY

archaeologist: a scientist who studies the remains of past cultures

artifact: a human-made object, especially one characteristic of a certain group or historical period

cast: to create objects by pouring melted metal into molds and allowing it to harden

domesticate: to adapt a plant or an animal to living with humans and to serving their purposes

engineer: a person who designs and builds machines, structures, and other objects

force: physical effort that causes an object to move or stop moving

friction: the force that slows motion when one surface rubs against another

fulcrum: the pivot point around which a lever turns in raising or moving an object

gear: a toothed wheel that transfers motion and power from one part of a machine to another

hominid: any of a family of two-footed primate mammals that include the human beings together with their extinct ancestors and related forms

irrigation: to supply water to farmland using channels, reservoirs, pumps, and other machines

machine: a device that does work by increasing or changing the direction of force

mechanical advantage: the degree to which a machine increases force

pivot: a shaft or pin on which something turns

prehistoric: of, relating to, or existing in times before written history

prime mover: a source of power (such as a windmill, waterwheel, or engine) designed to use force and motion from a natural source to drive machinery

pulley: a grooved wheel attached to a rope

reconstruction: to recreate or reimagine something, especially by using information acquired through research

relic: something from the past, especially after decay or disappearance

screw: a rod surrounded by a spiral ridge that works like an inclined plane

simple machines: six machines that form the basis for all other machines

smelt: to separate metal from ore by heating it in a furnace

wedge: a tool that is thicker at one end than at the other

wheel and axle: a simple machine in which a larger wheel is used to turn a smaller rod called an axle

work: the amount of energy needed to move an object over a particular distance

SOURCE NOTES

29   "inventor of the . . . hewn [cut] stone.": L. Sprague de Camp, *The Ancient Engineers* (Garden City, NY: Doubleday, 1963), 30.

29   "from the summit . . . ages behold you.": Antoine-Jean Gros, "Napoleon at the Battle of the Pyramids, July 21st, 1798" 1841, Prints, Drawings and Watercolors from the Anne S.K. Brown Military Collection, Brown Digital Repository, Brown University Library, https://repository.library.brown.edu/studio/item/bdr:245015/.

37   "On one occasion . . . of the instrument.": Peter James and Nick Thorpe, *Ancient Inventions* (New York: Ballantine, 1994), 143.

39   "[Their] arms consisted . . . our Spanish swords.": Bernal Diaz Del Castillo, *The Memoirs of the Conquistador Bernal Diaz del Castillo*, vol. 1. (London: J. Hatchard and Son, 1844), 231.

49   "Then at daybreak . . . of the enemy.": Diodorus Siculus, "The Library of History of Diodorus Siculus," available online from Bill Thayer, November 30, 2008, http://penelope.uchicago.edu/Thayer/E/Roman/Texts/Diodorus_Siculus/20D*.html.

55   "The ships were . . . was let fall.": Plutarch, *Plutarch's Lives*, Project Gutenberg, October 1996, https://gutenberg.org/files/674/674-h/674-h.htm.

61   "Wheels on rivers . . . to the top.": Marcus Vitruvius Pollio, *De Architectura*, book 10, available online from Bill Thayer, November 30, 2008, http://penelope.uchicago.edu/Thayer/E/Roman/Texts/Vitruvius/10*.html (May 14, 2010).

62   "Clever like none . . . construction of machines.": Robert James Forbes, *Studies in Ancient Technology*, vol. 2 (Leiden, Netherlands: E. J. Brill, 1993), 95.

SELECTED BIBLIOGRAPHY

Bunch, Bryan, and Alexander Hellemans. *The Timetables of Technology: A Chronology of the Most Important People and Events in the History of Technology*. New York: Simon & Schuster, 1993.

Diamond, Jared. *Guns, Germs, and Steel: The Fates of Human Societies*, 20th Anniversary ed. New York: W. W. Norton, 2017.

Fagen, Brian, ed. *Discovery! Unearthing the New Treasures of Archaeology*. London: Thames & Hudson, 2007.

Fagan, Brian. *The Seventy Great Inventions of the Ancient World*. London: Thames & Hudson, 2004.

Hackett, John. *Warfare in the Ancient World*. New York: Facts on File, 1989.

Hill, Donald. *A History of Engineering in Classical and Medieval Times*. London: Routledge, 1996.

Scarre, Chris. *Smithsonian Timelines of the Ancient World*. London: Dorling Kindersley, 1993.

Schick, Kathy D., and Nicholas Toth. *Making Silent Stones Speak: Human Evolution and the Dawn of Technology*. New York: Simon & Schuster, 1993.

Schiller, Ronald. *Distant Secrets: Unraveling the Mysteries of Our Ancient Past*. New York: Carol Publishing, 1989.

Soedel, Werner, and Vernard Foley. "Ancient Catapults." *Scientific American*, March 1979, 150–160.

Williams, Trevor I. *The History of Invention*. New York: Facts on File, 1987.

FURTHER READING

Books

Bridgeman, Roger. *1000 Inventions and Discoveries*. New York, NY: DK Publishing, 2020.
Take a tour through some of the most important discoveries in technology, medicine, and mathematics. From prehistoric tools to social media, learn the science behind inventions that changed human history.

Kenny, Karen Latchana. *Folding Tech: Using Origami and Nature to Revolutionize Technology*. Minneapolis: Twenty-First Century Books, 2021.
Discover how the ancient art of paper folding is inspiring today's technology in this in-depth look at the math and history behind folding technologies.

Macaulay, David. *The Way Things Work Now: From Levers to Lasers, Windmills to Wi-Fi*. Boston: Houghton Mifflin Harcourt, 2016.
Learn about the technology behind the machines we interact with every day, from 3D printers to jet airplanes. Discover how the engineering behind these machines works in this illustrated guide to the history of machines.

Miller, Tessa. *Wings & Beaks: Technology Inspired by Animals*. Minneapolis: Full Tilt Press, 2019.
From dragonfly drones to sonar, humans have been inspired to make new technologies mimicking flying creatures. This book shows how nature has inspired human machinery throughout history.

Woods, Mary B. and Michael. *Construction through the Ages*. Minneapolis: Twenty-First Century Books, 2025.
Machines throughout history have been used to construct everything from houses to monuments. Learn the history of ancient construction techniques and the technology behind them.

Websites

Roman Empire
> https://www.bbc.co.uk/bitesize/topics/zwmpfg8
> Learn about life in the Roman empire through this interactive website with in-depth education guides and information on the ancient world.

Rube Goldberg Machines
> https://www.rubegoldberg.org/
> Rube Goldberg was an artist and inventor who drew complicated machines that solved simple problems. Learn how you can create your own machine and submit it to the annual Rube Goldberg Machine Contest.

Seven Wonders of the Ancient World
> https://education.nationalgeographic.org/resource/resource-library-ancient-egypt
> Created by National Geographic, this site offers interactive features and up-to-date news about the pyramids and other wonders of ancient Egypt.

Simple Machines
> https://www.khanacademy.org/science/physics/discoveries/simple-machines-explorations/a/simple-machines-and-how-to-use-this-tutorial
> This tutorial from Khan Academy explores the six simple machines and the mathematics behind them through fun, interactive videos and activities.

INDEX

ABOUT THE AUTHORS

Michael Woods is a science and medical journalist in Washington, DC. He has won many national writing awards. Mary B. Woods is a school librarian. Their past books include the fifteen–volume *Disasters Up Close* series and many titles in the *Seven Wonders* series. The Woodses have four children. When not writing, reading, or enjoying their seven grandchildren, the Woodses travel to gather material for future books.

PHOTO ACKNOWLEDGMENTS